A Radioman's Journey Through World War II
and His Cartoons That Told the Story

The USS Colusa APA 74 bringing Troops Home After World War II
Photo # NH 98711 USS Colusa in San Francisco Bay circa 1945-46

by Navy Veteran, Radioman 3rd Class, Cartoonist, and Architect
Milton A. Lockett

A Radioman's Journey through World War II and His Cartoons That Told the Story

by Milton Ambrose Lockett

with Sharon Marshall Lockett

© 2020 Milton Ambrose Lockett

Lockett Learning Systems

All rights reserved. No part of this book may be reproduced without written permission from Lockett Learning Systems.

www.LockettLearningSystems.com

www.MALockettBuildingDesign.com

Library of Congress Cataloging Data

Lockett, Milton Ambrose, 1926-

    A Radioman's Journey Through World War II...

    and His Cartoons That Told the Story

    Milton Ambrose Lockett with

    Sharon Marshall Lockett

    ISBN 13: 978-1-931001-41-0

    1. World War II. 2. World War II Pacific Theatre.

    3. World War II Navy Memoirs. 4. Military Humor

Cover Design by Dr. Carol Mattson

Dedication

This book is lovingly dedicated to my wife,
Sharon Marshall Lockett,
who compiled and organized the information
and remains both my best friend
and my greatest fan.

A special thanks goes to the editors who tirelessly read,
critiqued, suggested, and corrected the copy:

Velda Rose

Carol Mattson, EdD

A Radioman's Journey Through World War II
and His Cartoons that Told the Story

Introduction	vii
Foreword	**1**
Milt's Journey, In His Words	1
Welcome Aboard	**3**
Boot Camp and Radio School	4
The Morse Code	5
12 Cartoons About Life Aboard the USS Colusa	9
A Sailor's Work	**35**
Radio Operator, USS Colusa, APA 74	36
19 Cartoons About The Work On Board	39
Time Off	**77**
Fun Times	78
Rites of Passage	79
16 Cartoons About Leave and Leisure	81
The War	**113**
The Great War As Seen From the Navy	114
The Code Talkers	114
Rationing	117
10 Cartoons Related to The Reason We're Here	119
Official Telegram: The War Is Over!	138
V-J Day Celebrations	139
Occupation of Japan	140
World War II Key Dates	141
Welcome Home	**143**
Homeward Bound	144
Life After the Navy	144
20 Cartoons About Adjusting to Life Stateside	147
About the Cartoonist	**187**

Introduction

by Sharon Marshall Lockett

We were decorating our home with memorabilia to celebrate Milt's 90th Birthday when we ran across a national treasure: his Navy cartoons from World War II. I knew he was a gifted architect. I didn't know he had ever drawn cartoons. I was mesmerized. I still am.

This began our trek to share his gift with you. The originals were yellowed with age, fragile, and disorganized. We organized them and copied them in black and white. What you see has not been touched up; it reflects his original work at age 18...even more poignant because he drew them on an old mimeograph sheet, which meant he could not make corrections.

Once copied, we began the process of jarring his memory of events 75 years ago. Each **Section Introduction** contains his memories of the related events. The process of writing his **"Artist's Reflection,"** placed on the page to the left of each cartoon, was captivating. The detail and symbolism in his work astonish me. I am more in awe of his talent every time I see it.

Along with the reflections, we share some articles from the ship's newspaper. These are labeled **FUBAR** (the paper's name: Fidelity, Unity, Bravery, Allegiance, Readiness). They are obviously from an old non-electric typewriter. Some that are poignant but difficult to read have been re-typed but not edited...and still bear the label FUBAR.

You will often see the title: **Did You Know....** This section brings historical facts to light that are pertinent to the cartoon or time period. Many items came from Internet research. If one source said it so uniquely I was intrigued, the source is noted. If the information was readily available from multiple sources, it is not. Other items in this section came from my questions to him as we explored the meaning behind a cartoon. That means the memories are 75 years old. He is pretty amazing, but 75 years is a long time. If there are discrepancies between his recall and your research, please forgive us. If it is major, please contact us and it will be corrected for the next edition.

The cartoons are grouped into five sections: *Welcome Aboard, A Sailor's Work, Time Off, The War,* and *Welcome Home,* followed by a narrative of his recollections on the topic. The cover pages to these sections he drew at age 92. The cartoons he drew at ages 18 and 19 do not contain his by-line, but his current ones do. I think you will agree he still has it!

Sometimes the Colusa would transport a serviceman who also loved to draw. A few cartoons were drawn by them and are labeled "guest artists." We have tried but have been unable to identify or locate them. If you recognize their work, please tell us. They will be given their deserved credit in future editions of this book and on social media.

Compiling this made me realize how little I know about "the great war" and how I wish I had studied history more fervently in school. I learned more about history through this project than I ever did as a student in the classroom. I also gained insight and perspective quite different from what I was taught.

One more thing...this has been a labor of love. I loved and admired him as a husband, friend, and architect before we started. My admiration for him has mushroomed through this compilation. So much of what shaped him happened before I knew him. I am grateful it helped him grow into a man of integrity and character. I am reminded of the words by Robert Browning, penned so many years ago:

> *"Grow old along with me! The best is yet to be, the last of life, for which the first was made. Our times are in his hand who saith, 'A whole I planned, youth shows but half; Trust God: See all, nor be afraid'!"*

I am honored to grow old with this man. I am in awe of his talent. I am his partner in life and in this project. He draws pictures. I write books!

Enjoy!

Milt and Sharon Lockett
2017

Foreword

Milt's Journey, In His Words

Milton Ambrose Lockett
Radioman III
1944, age 17

World War II was raging, and patriotism was high. As a recruiting incentive, high school juniors and seniors were given the option of earning a high school diploma by joining the military their senior year instead of taking the traditional high school graduation requirements. A friend and I decided we should join the Navy. I went from high school senior and cheerleader to enlisted man overnight. I soon discovered that my buddy changed his mind; I was on my own.

I began my tour of duty with the US Navy on April 21, 1944. I was 17 years old and a high school senior. Because I was under age, I had to have my parents' signatures to join. I graduated from Narbonne High School (Lomita, California) with my class on June 23, 1944, wearing my uniform instead of the traditional cap and gown. It was a great day; everyone cheered when I walked forward to receive my diploma. I was the only graduate wearing a military uniform instead of a cap and gown. I was the first person in my family to graduate from high school.

Milton Ambrose Lockett
Architect
2019, Age 92

12 Cartoons About Life Aboard the USS Colusa

Boot Camp and Radio School:

As a new recruit, I traveled by train from Los Angeles to San Diego for Boot Camp. I had never been on a train before so that alone was exciting. After eight weeks of Boot Camp, the Navy assigned me to attend radio school in Los Angeles, California.

About 20 of us started Radio School, which lasted about six months. We learned the Morse Code "dots" (.) and "dashes" (-) and trained with head phones learning to transcribe messages. Only one of the recruits didn't finish. One day he threw down his head phones and ran out saying, "I can't stand this any more!"

I graduated from Radio School on October 6, 1944. I was assigned to work as a radioman on the USS Colusa, a troop transport ship serving in the South Pacific.

Artist's Reflection:

The Morse Code is an artifact of history.
It has been replaced by newer technology.

I last used the Morse Code in 1946 when
I was in the Navy.

I never forgot it.
I could send any message
in Morse Code today.

The Morse Code:

The Morse code was used as an international standard for maritime distress until 1999 when it was replaced by the Global Maritime Distress Safety System. The ship's messages came in Morse Code in groups of 4 letters and a space. After we typed them, they looked something like this:

ABCD	CBMB	PQRS	TUVD
LGMN	OTSB	RPSQ	GMQV
FLDQ	OPRT	YVDA	QMVC
RSTP	XLCV	YOVX	PRVA
RPLQ	GOVP	YESP	HRBW

We fed the groups of four letters into a decoder machine and out came a message. Every country had a unique code. Our messages usually came from either San Francisco or Manila. Those that came from Manila were really fast, like 60 to 70 words per minute in Morse Code. When it came out that fast, it was almost like someone was talking to you.

SOS was originally established for maritime use to signal distress and call for help. In Morse Code, it is three dots, three dashes, three dots:

$$\cdots \quad --- \quad \cdots$$

Although the Morse Code has not been used for many years, SOS is still used as an internationally-recognized standard distress signal.

Here is an example of my name as it would look in Morse Code:

m:	--		**l:**	.-..
i:	..		**o:**	---
l:	.-..		**c:**	-.-.
t:	-		**k:**	-.-
o:	---		**e:**	.
n:	-.		**t:**	-
			t:	-

It would come to me in code and might look something like this after I would type it:

OQVD YSPG MVOD D

The decoder would translate the grouped letters:
Milton Lockett

Did You Know...

When the French Navy ceased using Morse code on January 31, 1997, the final message transmitted read:

"Calling all. This is our last cry before our eternal silence."

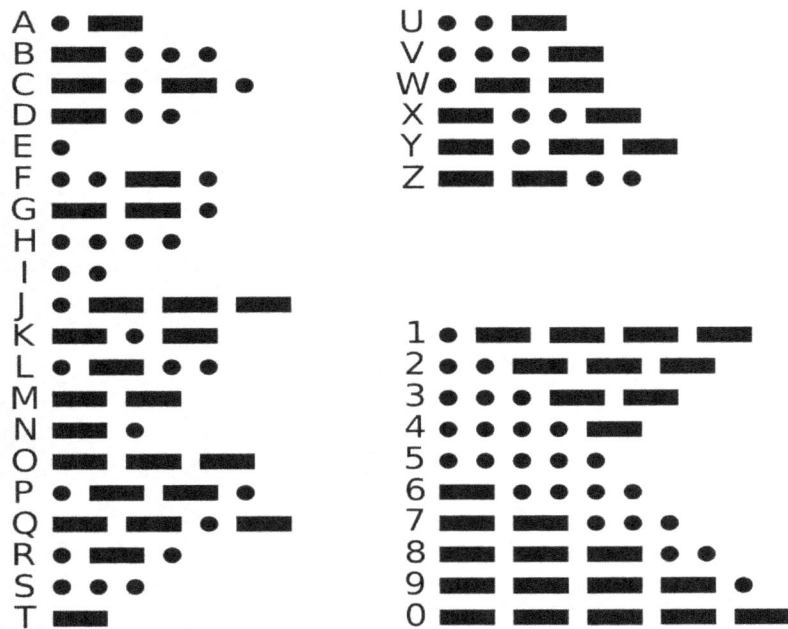

Undated

Artist's Reflection

It was easy to brag
to our girlfriends,
but many men
spent their first few
days or weeks on board
battling sea sickness.

How It Really Was!

March 15, 1945

Artist's Reflection:

This guy was trying to find the laundry
so he could get his clothes washed.

Instead, he found the engine room.
It was easy to get lost on such a massive ship.

Did You Know?

The USS Colusa was commissioned on October 7, 1944, in San Pedro, California. She was decommissioned May 15, 1946.

The ship was staffed with 27 officers and 293 enlisted men. On an average trip, she carried troops of 47 officers and 802 enlisted men.

Her many decks were 427 feet long–longer than a football field.

Lost On Board

October 7, 1945

Artist's Reflection:

We were in the South Pacific.
It was hot and humid on the ship.
We didn't have air conditioning.
The wind was blowing
but it wasn't cool where we were.

Bunks were four high.

In this guy's room, he imagines laying on
a block of ice under a fan.

It was pretty miserable.
Our division bunks were two decks down.
They pumped air through an air duct.
I tried to reach my hand over,
hoping the air was cool,
and direct it to me.

Hot and Humid

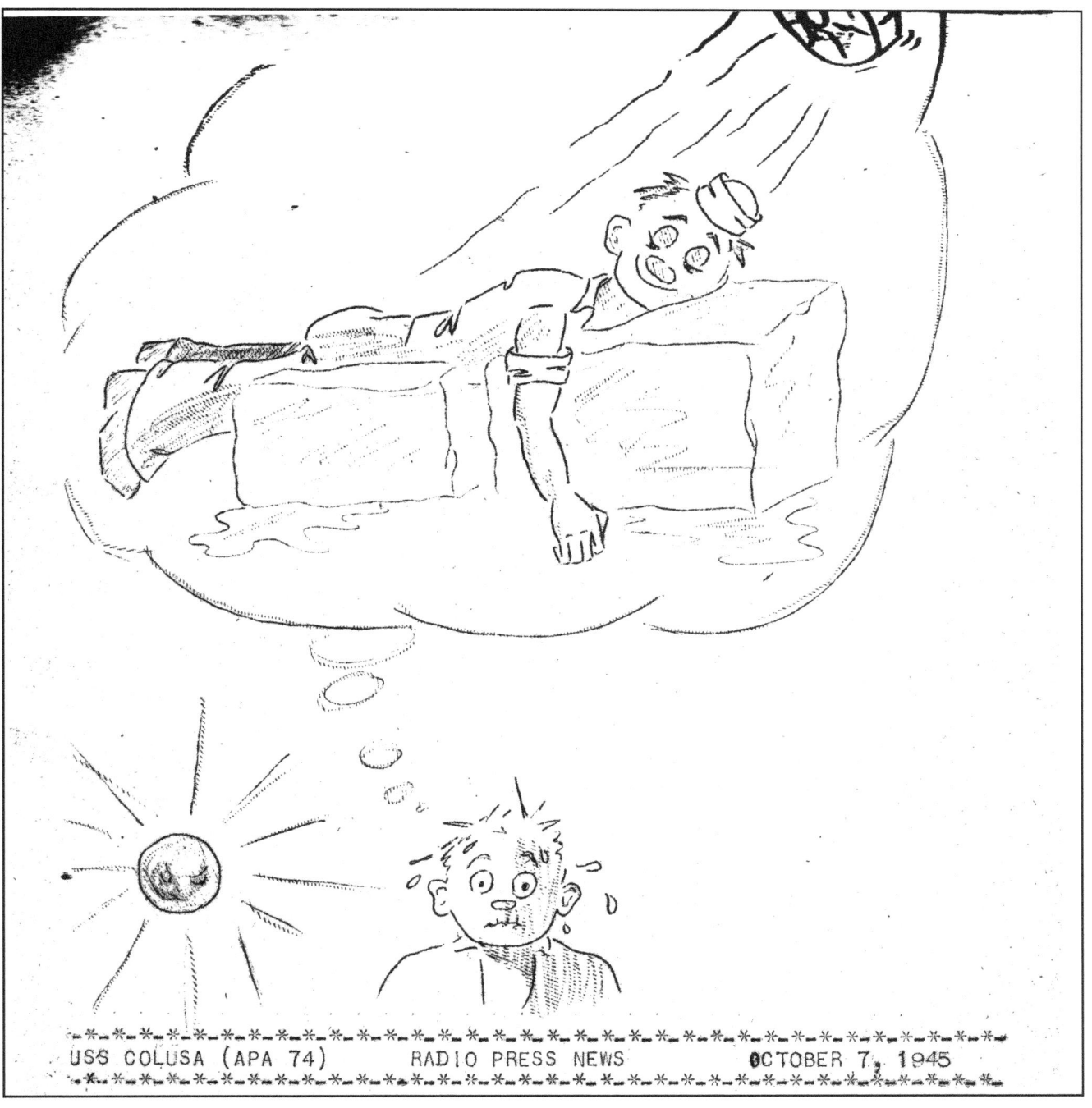

Guest Artist . Undated

Artist's Reflection

We didn't have refrigerated drinks on the ship.

Even our beer and sodas were lukewarm.

When we went off-ship for any reason,
people apologized if their drinks weren't sparkling cold.

To us, even warm tasted good.

Guest Artist . Just a Cup of Water

*With my apologies, I don't know the name of this guest artist. I included the work in appreciation for the encouragement and camaraderie we shared. If you recognize the work, please let us know. We will credit the artist in future editions.

July 1, 1945

Artist's Reflection:

*Every week on board
we got an "allowance,"
a certain number of "chits"
that we could spend on board
for beer or snacks.*

*They looked like tickets and were dated.
This guy was trying to buy beer with
last week's chits.*

*I don't think anyone ever really
forgot to spend what they had!*

Did You Know...

A chit in the Navy refers to any piece of paper from a form to a pass and even currency. According to the Navy History Museum, the word chit was carried over from the days of Hindu traders when they used slips of paper called "citthi" for money.

No Sale!

August 5, 1945

Artist's Reflection:

Although many African Americans
served faithfully during World War II,
on the ship most were relegated to stewards' mates (waiters)
who served food to the officers.

They were segregated and
all bunked together on the lower decks.

We have made strides to improve such blatant discrimination.
We have much work yet to be done.
We must not be content until
"all men are created (and treated) equal..."

Did You Know?

During World War II, 167,000 African Americans served in the Navy, initially as mess attendants and cooks. In 1942, general service was opened for African-Americans to serve in other capacities. In March 1944, the first thirteen African-American naval officers were commissioned. One of the first heroes of the war was Ship's Cook Third Class Doris Miller, from Waco, Texas, aboard the USS West Virginia at Pearl Harbor December 7, 1941. His Navy Cross citation reads in part:

Discrimination against black people who have served in the U.S. military lasted from its creation during the Revolutionary War to the end of segregation by President Harry S. Truman's Executive Order 9981 in 1948.

Hot and Stuffy

'Those who cannot remember the past are condemned to repeat it.' (George Santayana-1905). In a 1948 speech to the House of Commons, Winston Churchill changed the quote slightly when he said (paraphrased), 'Those who fail to learn from history are condemned to repeat it.'

Undated

Artist's Reflection

*Our ship had air
blowing in through the vents...*

But it wasn't refrigerated.

*We spent long hours being hot and humid,
Dreaming of better weather.*

Still Hot

September 11, 1945

Artist's Reflection:

*Sinks, toilets, mirrors, and showers
were all in one big open room.*

On one wall would be sinks and mirrors.

*The next wall had a trough with
a row of toilet seats on top.*

*On the other wall was a
row of showers.*

*It could get pretty crowded
and smelly.*

Where's The Soap?

April 4, 1945

Artist's Reflection:

This guy is lucky!
The 50 cents he found will get him liberty
at the Pepsi Cola Center.

The two half circles you see in the background
make a toilet seat,
and the room has several seats in a row.

We sat down with others to
do our business.
The salt water came in one end of the trough and
ran out the other,
washing out our debris with it.

I always tried to sit on the high end!

The Everything Room

March 2, 1945

Artist's Reflection:

It's chow time.
They're hungry.

There were always people who complained
about the food.
I thought the food was good
even when there were bugs in it!

(We were gone for a long time
and the food often had bugs in it).

I was a young, hungry man
and food was food.

Did You Know...

The ship's crews were on duty 24 hours a day. To accommodate the rotating shifts over a 24-hour period, the staff served approximately 1200 meals four times a day, seven days a week. That's 33,600 meals a week.

Melee

Undated

Artist's Reflection

*Our mouths watered as we
watched the delivery truck unload
bringing us bags of good food.*

*It didn't look the same on our trays
in the mess hall.*

*My first Saturday of Basic Training, we marched
from our Barracks down the "Grinder"
(the pavement area where we practiced marching)
to the Mess Hall.
It seemed like a long march.
When we got there, we were starving.
We got a big plate of beans for breakfast.*

*On Saturday mornings,
we always got a plate of beans for breakfast.*

*They were very good, but
Who got the ham?*

Who Got The Ham?

Undated

Artist's Reflection

*The tables in the mess hall
were like picnic benches
with seats on both sides.*

*Sometimes the sea was very rough,
and it would literally
knock your trays off the table.*

*We had to hold onto the tray with one hand
and eat with the other.*

That's All

July 4, 1945

Artist's Reflection:

It didn't matter what they served.
I always liked the food...
but...

when we were at sea for several months,
the food switched from fresh to
canned, dried, or pickled.

I especially remember docking in San Francisco.
The supply clerks stood as we disembarked
handing each of us a big head of lettuce.

We ate it whole,
savoring the taste of fresh.

Iceberg is still my favorite lettuce.

Did You Know...

The armed forces always tried to serve balanced meals to the men, knowing they needed their health and strength.

Special Independence Day Menu

U.S.S. COLUSA APA-74

INDEPENDENCE DAY

MENU

JULY 4   1945

CREAM OF TOMATO SOUP
CRACKERS

ROAST CHICKEN   BAKED SPICED HAM

GIBLET GRAVY

GREEN OLIVES   SWEET PICKLES

MASHED POTATOES   BUTTERED LIMA BEANS

BUTTERED CORN

LETTUCE AND TOMATO SALAD   MAYONNAISE

APPLE CRUMB PIE

ICE CREAM   HOT ROLLS

HARD CANDY

BREAD   BUTTER

LEMONADE

CIGARS   CIGARETTES

ALEXANDER DONEGAN   W.S. DALE   D.W. SWANGER
LIEUT. COMDR. USNR   CCS USN   Lieut. (jg) SC, USNR
COMMANDING OFFICER   SUPPLY OFFICER

19 Cartoons About The Work Day

Radio Operator, USS Colusa, APA 74.

After Radio School, I was assigned to the USS Colusa, APA 74 in Los Angeles Harbor. The Colusa was an Attack Transport designated to move troops to and from the battlefield. Our ship carried landing crafts to deliver troops to the South Pacific Islands where we were assigned. Typically, we left our home base in San Francisco with a load of 800 or 900 military servicemen plus our ship's company. We unloaded the troops in Hawaii. We left Hawaii with new troops to transport them to some islands we captured from the Japanese. We would bring the troops to the island, pick up the wounded troops from the invasion, and go back to Pearl Harbor to repeat the route with a new group of fresh troops and returning wounded. We traveled north to Alaska and south to Australia.

I served as a radio operator and received the messages through a set of ear phones. There were several radiomen on the ship. We worked 4-hour shifts with 8 hours off. All of the messages received on the ship came in Morse code at 30 to 70 words per minute, in groups of four letters. We listened through ear phones as the message came through as a radio transmission. Our job was to transcribe the messages using a typewriter...an old-fashioned typewriter without power, memory, or auto-correct. What I transcribed was in code; it didn't make sense so we fed it to a decoding machine to translate it into a readable message.

Vintage Typewriter like the one I used

As radio operators, we were also in charge of writing the ship's newspaper. I loved to draw, so soon I began creating cartoons for the ship's newspaper named FUBAR (Fidelity, Unity, Bravery, Allegiance, Recognition). I enjoyed this fun project and, evidently, was good at it. In fact, the crew enjoyed my work so much that they created souvenir packages of the cartoons. Once a passenger on board from the Marines looked at my cartoons and told me to apply for a job at Disney when I was discharged; he had worked there.

The newspaper and cartoons were drawn on a mimeograph stencil. Using something akin to a stylus, we would draw and/or type on the stencil. To make shading on the images, we used a little roller. My first strokes were used because I couldn't erase or write over on a stencil. Wherever a pen touched, a hole was made. The machine had ink in its drum which filled the holes to make the printed image.

Mimeograph Machine with
Stencils like we used
to publish the ship's newspaper

March 8, 1945

Artist's Reflection:

The name of our newspaper was

FUBAR:

Fidelity, Unity, Bravery, Allegiance, Readiness

We sailors nicknamed it

Fouled

Up

Beyond

All

Recognition.

This guy was painting our sign.

Did You Know...

Part of our job as radiomen was to publish a daily newspaper which included updates from the war, personal news from the crew, humor, imaginative articles, and cartoons. It was intended to build camaraderie and morale.

FUBAR

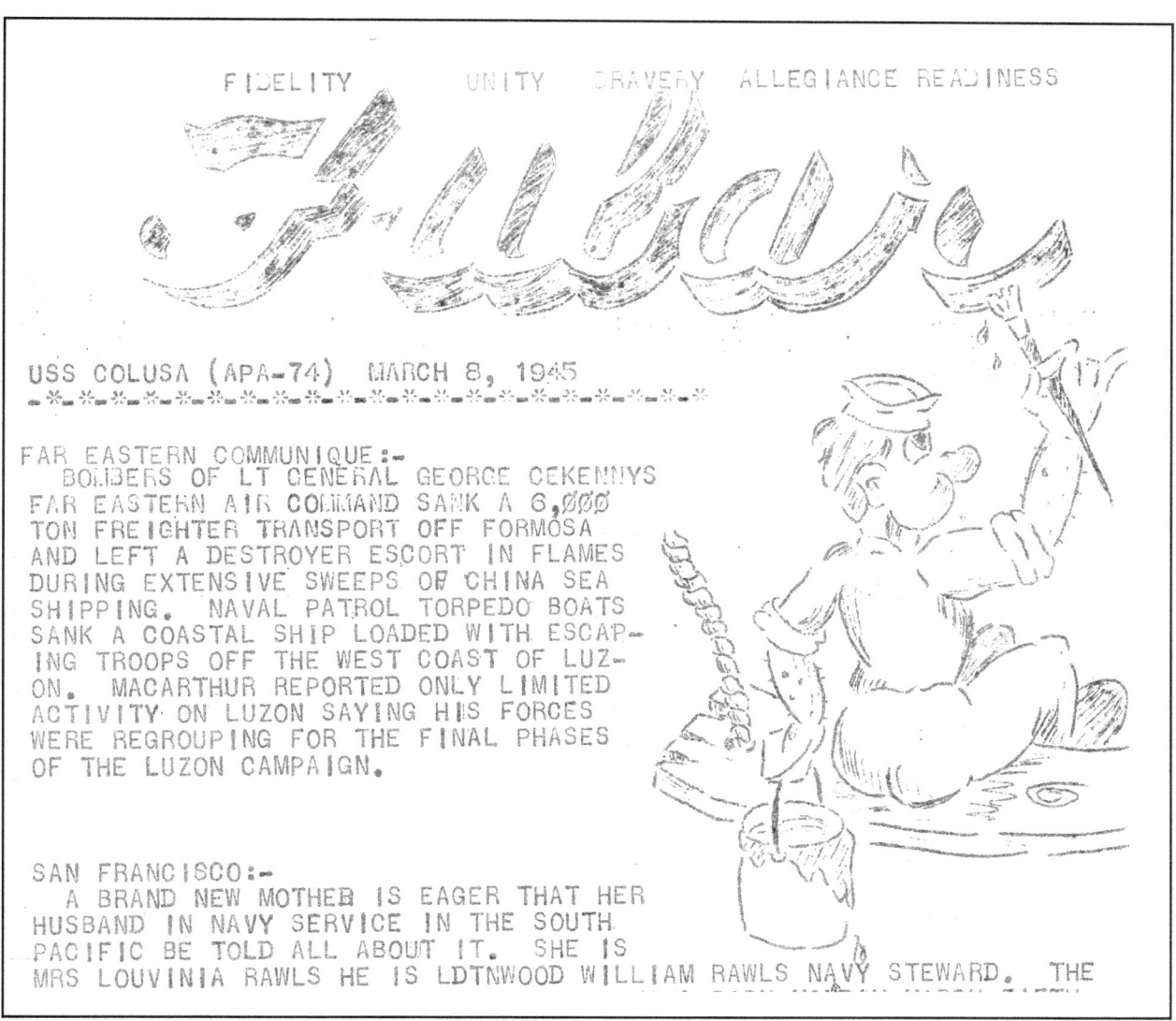

Undated

Artist's Reflection

"Some day I'm going to murder the bugler."

Every morning, the bugler awoke us to "Reveille."
Every evening we went to sleep to the sound of "Taps."

Notice the bunks were 4 high.
At the end of each row were groups of
lockers where we stored all our personal belongings.

There were 4 rows of bunks, each 4 high,
one on each side and two in the middle.
About 100 beds were grouped together in each sleeping area.
At any given time, we housed 800 to 1,000 troops and staff.
Mine was a bottom bunk.

Did You Know...

Shortly after being drafted in 1918, Irving Berlin composed the well-known and oft-quoted song "Oh, how I hate to get up in the morning." It was his protest against the indignities of military routines.

Reveille!

Undated

Artist's Reflection

Every Saturday was considered inspection time.
We were expected to have our bunks made and wrinkle free.
Our ship quarters were to be clean.

While we were at sea, the inspections were more lax.
These inspectors are enjoying the pin-ups.

SAT Inspection

Undated

Artist's Reflection

We were constantly painting somewhere on the ship.

Did You Know...

Swabbie is a term used to describe a Navy enlisted man. It is derived from one of their common duties, "swabbing the deck."

Wet Paint

Guest Artist . Undated

Artist's Reflection

We were just kids.
The oldest seaman on board was probably not yet 25.

We thought we were
men so we did our jobs.
Men don't ask for directions!

*With my apologies, I don't know the name of this guest artist. I included the work in appreciation for the encouragement and camaraderie we shared. If you recognize the work, please let us know. We will credit the artist in future editions.

Guest Artist . Ship Repairs

March 11, 1945

Artist's Reflection:

We worked hard scrubbing the deck
on the ship.

Pepper, our Cocker and mascot,
was laid back enjoying his bone
and supervising the workers.

The swabbies say, "Goldbrick!"
That means he's loafing and
not doing his part.

Did You Know...

Many U.S. military units in World War II adopted animal mascots. Though traditionally considered bearers of good luck, these mascots were really pets who belonged to all the men of a squad, company, or ship. They were greatly loved.

It's a Dog's Life

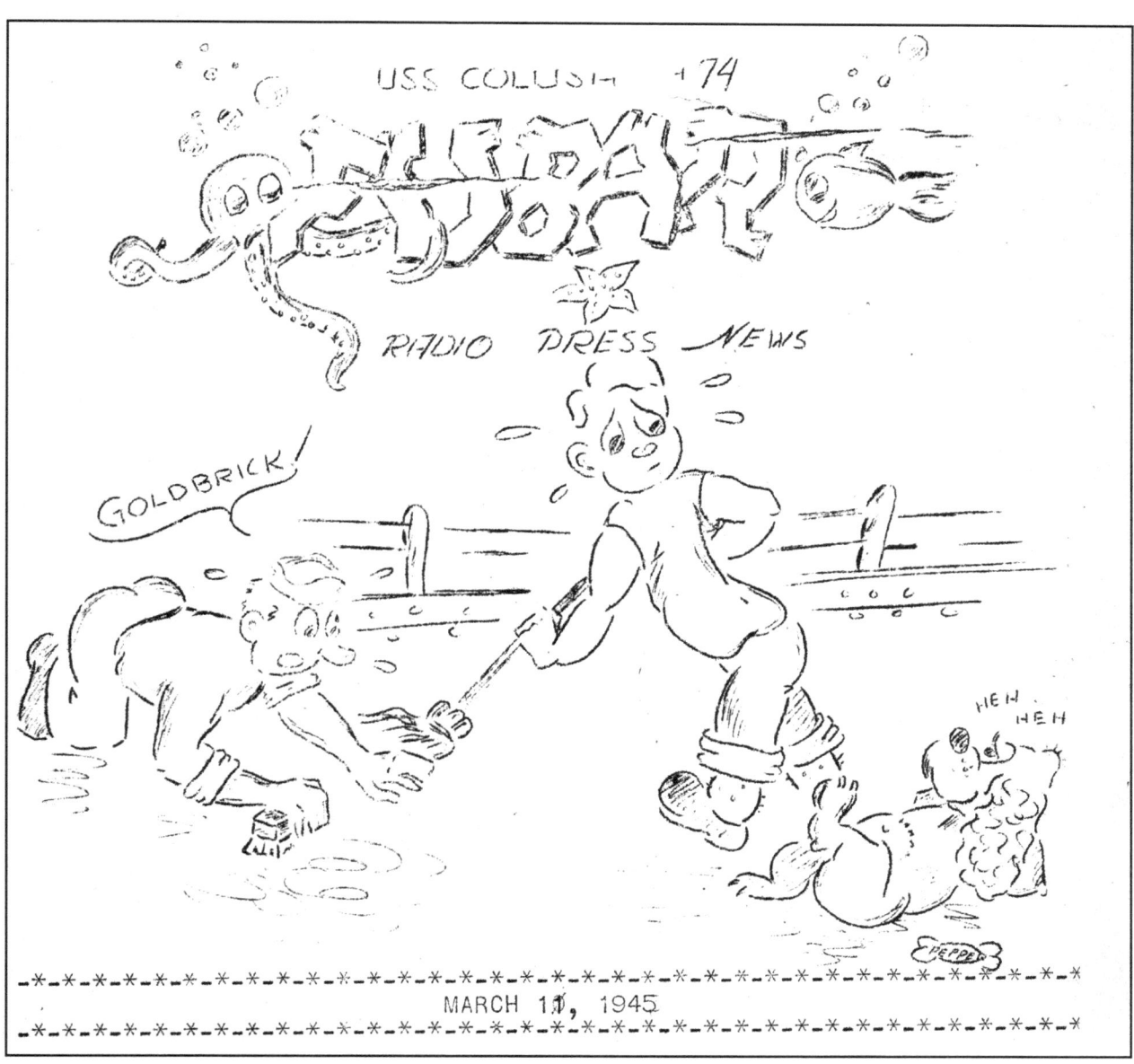

March 16, 1945

Artist's Reflection:

We're going ashore on an island shortly.

Pepper, our cocker and mascot,
is dreaming of the trees.

The swabbie is dreaming of girls.

Swabbies were always dreaming of girls
and missing the girls back home.

Dreaming

June 27, 1945

Much of our time on board was spent
keeping the ship in "ship shape."

The deck had just been painted,
and here came Pepper the dog
defiantly walking right through
all the wet paint!

Wet Paint

Undated

Artist's Reflection

The Electrician's Mate brought his Cocker Spaniel on board.
Everyone loved her.
Her name was Pepper, and
she became our ship Mascot.

One day she fell over the side of the ship.
We turned the entire ship around
looking for her
but never found her.

Rest in Peace, Pepper!

RIP Pepper

Undated

Artist's Reflection

We lost an anchor.

Gone American League

July 9, 1945

Artist's Reflection:

It's a Drill!
Man Your Battle Stations!

Guys are running in from all directions...
some fresh from the shower,
some climbing the walls.

The floor has just been painted.
Some are tripping over the rope that says
Wet Paint!

I was getting discharged when an
announcement came over the speaker saying,
"N Division, Hit The Decks!"

This was my division being called to paint the decks.
I was spared.

Man Your Battle Stations

Undated

Artist's Reflection

We had doctors and a hospital.

There were so many things
to interfere with concentration...
rocking ship, beautiful seascape...

I'm glad I never needed
surgery on board!

Did You Know...

Hospitals on board Troop Transport ships were known as Sick Bays. Policy was for the wounded to receive surgery within 12 hours of an injury. Hospital ships could only come after the battle area had been secured. Sometimes that would take several days or weeks. That made it imperative that troop transport ships treat those who needed immediate care. Triage of the wounded required those who needed surgery to be carried to the sick bay, and the less wounded were sent to battle stations on the ship. Corpsmen and medical officers worked meticulously to overcome the challenges of needing to operate on board.

Source: https://www.anesthesiahistoryjournal.org/article/S2352-4529(18)30018-5/pdf

So Many Distractions

September 17, 1945

Artist's Reflection:

We were docked and there were great big swells.

It rolled so bad it looked like you could walk up the wall,
to the rest room and the chow hall.

It was rolling so bad you could hardly walk.

The big swells in the ocean often rocked us
about 70°,
even when we were anchored or docked.

A Little Rough

Undated

Artist's Reflection

We flew kites
and the gunners used them
for target practice.

Let's Go Fly a Kite

March 19, 1945

Artist's Reflection:

We were a troop transport.
We loaded up a group of Marines.

They were used to destroying
anything that got in their way.

On a Navy ship, destruction wasn't king.

Navy 1, Marines 0

Did You Know?

During World War II, the branches of military included Army and Air Force, Navy, Marines, and Coast Guard. The Navy often transported military from all branches to and from their assigned battle grounds.

Navy 1 Marines 0

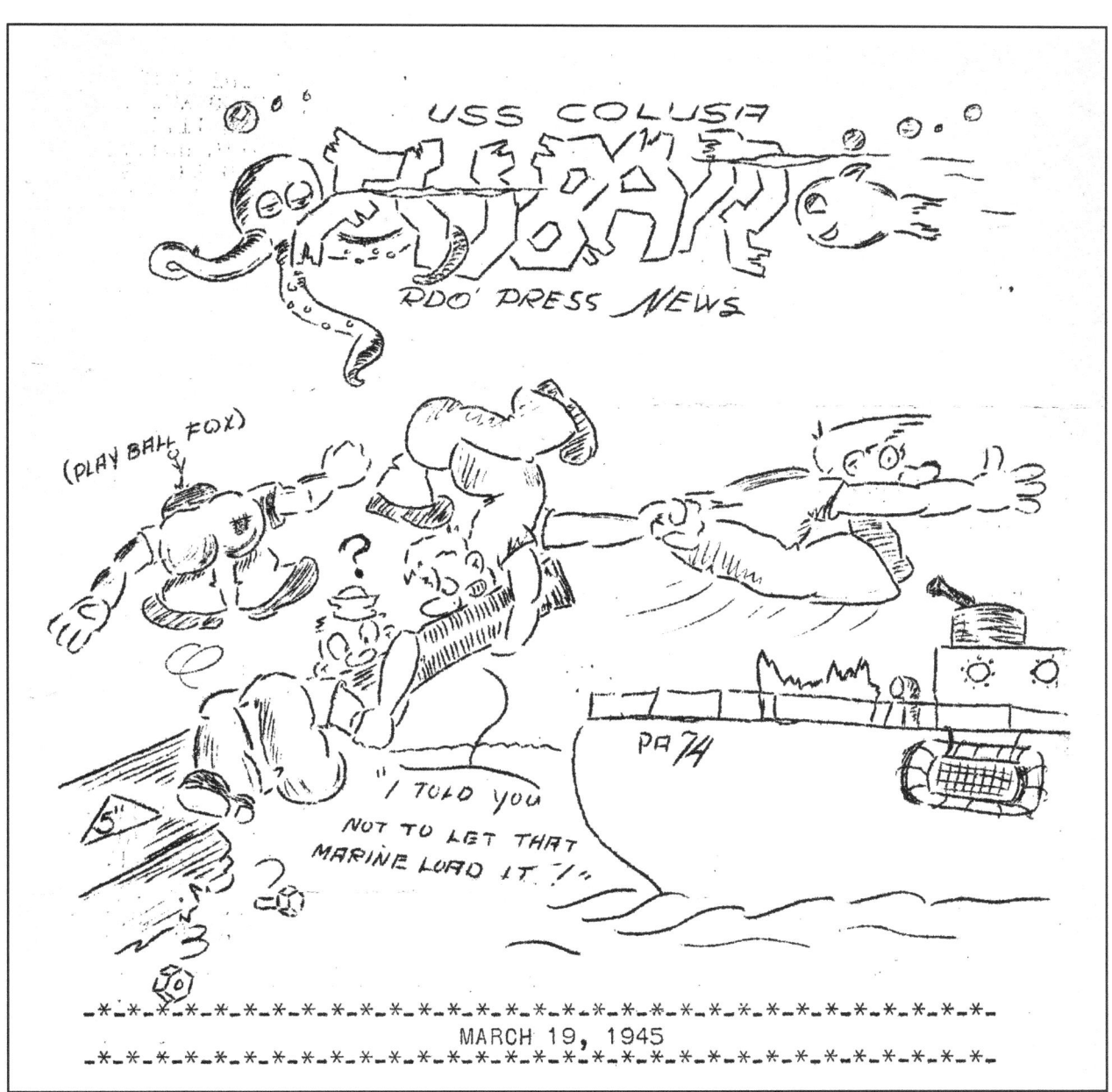

Undated

Artist's Reflection

We had "Smokers" on the ship.
The referee was accidently punched
in one of them.

We held boxing matches,
sometimes with
the ship's company
versus
the troops we were transporting.

Did You Know...

"Smoker" boxing matches were an important part of Navy life. It didn't take much in terms of equipment, organization, or athletic ability to host a boxing match, but it went a long way in promoting a good time, good morale, and esprit de corps.

Boxing Games

Round by round they fight their way
Until the third and final fray,
But when it's over 'tis plain to see
The loser is the referee.

JCT

Undated

Artist's Reflection

You name it,
we had it on board:
those who wanted out at any cost...
and those who did not want to go home
to whatever was awaiting them.

Did You Know...

The point system, called the Advanced Service Rating Score, had the objective of achieving equity in the demobilization. Soldiers were given one point for each month of military service and one additional point for each month of overseas service. Each battle star or decoration earned a soldier 5 points.

Future Lifer?

August 10, 1945

Artist's Reflection:

You earned points to get discharged.
You got points for several things like
how long you had been in,
if you were in combat,
if you had a wife and kids, etc.

So this guy sits there,
An old man with the pipe and everything.

They say "Did you hear?
He is finally getting discharged.
He has his 54 points!"

FUBAR Headlines:

MORE   POINTS

WASHINGTON-- THE NAVY LIBERALIZED ITS POINT SYSTEM TO GRANT ONE QUARTER OF A POINT FOR EVERY MONTHS SERVICE OUTSIDE THE CONTINENTAL LIMITS OF THE UNITED STATES SINCE SEPTEMBER 1, 1939. THE CHANGE WILL MAKE AN ADDITIONAL 423,000 PERSONNEL ELIGIBLE FOR DISCHARGE WHEN IT GOES INTO EFFECT ON SEPTEMBER 15TH, SECRETARY OF NAVY FORRESTAL ESTIMATED SIXTY PERCENT OF THOSE ELIGIBLE ARE OVERSEAS.

Short Timer

July 7, 1945

Artist's Reflection:

This guy is the Maxwell Klinger*
of World War II.

He just wants to go home!

What excuse shall it be this time?

I'm getting married?
My home burned down?
I'm getting divorced?
Grandma died?

Did You Know...

*Actor Jamie Farr starred as Maxwell Clinger on the MASH sitcom, popular on CBS from 1973 to 1983. He was always dreaming up a scheme to get a discharge.

Honorable Discharge

16 Cartoons About Leave and Leisure

Fun Times.

We felt so adult fighting the great war, but we were really just kids. Most of us were 18 to 21 years old. We always found a way to make life memorable and fun.

We spent holidays on board ship without much regalia except for a special dinner. Our loved ones at home didn't know where we were. Celebrations and presents waited until we returned home.

Two special "rites of passage" were crossing the international date line and crossing the equator. Those who had been there before would make a pit with cold water and throw us in. When we got out, they would stand in line to give us a swat. Once we were initiated into the Neptune society, we got to participate in the swatting. The last to go got the most swattings.

Here I Am
Aboard Ship, Christmas, 1945

Did You Know...

The Line Crossing Ceremony "Order of Neptune" observes a mariner's transformation from a slimy Pollywog (a seaman who hasn't crossed the equator) to a trusty Shellback, also called a son of Neptune.

Maritime personnel who crossed the point where the Equator crosses the International Date Line are called Golden Shellbacks.

Rites of Passage

Crossing the Equator
The Two-day Ceremony Was Big and Exciting
November, 1945

Here I am
Joining the Neptune Society

March 13, 1945

Artist's Reflection:

The Boot Camp instructors told us
that bars are the same all over the world.
Instead of spending our time in bars,
we should take advantage of our time
in the service to see the world:
go to new places,
visit new countries,
explore the cities.

We didn't see land for weeks at a time.
Coming ashore we can have
booze, girls, and palm trees.
The welcome mat is far better
than being out at sea.
We've been there for a long time,
and we're going back soon.
We need some recreation now.

It's hard to remember what the instructors said.

Out of Bounds

June 28, 1945

Artist Reflection:

*Midway Island was so small
we could sail right by and not see it.*

*At the time, I didn't know what the big deal was
because it was just a little island,
but it was a strategic one.*

*One of our nicknames for
Midway Island
was Half Way.*

*We always brought food for the island's cows
that provided milk for the troops*

Did You Know...

The Midway Island battle was June 3-6, 1942. It was one of the big turning points in World War II. The Japanese attacked Midway with their aircraft carriers. We sank three of their carriers; they sank one of ours. To the Japanese, that was a big dent in their Navy. They didn't capture Midway. It is strategically located roughly equidistant between North America and Asia. Today Midway Atoll is an unorganized, unincorporated territory of the United States.

~~Mid~~ Halfway

March 18, 1945

Artist's Reflection:

*When we landed on an island
and had a little free time,
We would often have a beer party
and enjoy the many pleasures
of the island.*

**R and R on Midway Island
I took the photo so I'm not in it; 1945**

Fun in the Sun

Undated

Artist's Reflection

When we were on liberty,
we were able to use our landing craft
as a pleasure vehicle.

Water skiing was a fun past time.

Too much coconut water could
give you diarrhea.

Did You Know...

As a troop transport ship, our landing crafts delivered new troops to the war zone and wounded to hospitals for medical treatment.

During liberty we were free to use them for fun.

Time to Play

July 3, 1945

Artist's Reflection:

Ashore in Australia,
our greatest obstacles
were the Gooney Birds!

They would chase you and bite.
They were funny.

FUBAR Humor:

```
"There are strange things done
       on the Gooney Bird run;
 The Cruise is smooth and fine,
 But Beware! Beware! my sailor lad,
--------Don't trip on a two inch line."
```

Did You Know...

Gooney Birds (Albatross) today are protected residents on Midway Atoll. They dwell primarily on islands in the Pacific.

Gooney Bird Run

April 3, 1945

Artist's Reflection:

*A local radio station
offered cash for answering
questions correctly.*

*This guy is trying to skip
the question part
and just take the cash.*

I'll Take The Cash

April 6, 1945

Artist's Reflection:

He's on liberty in San Francisco.
He wants to be sure
he gets back to the ship
but he doesn't want to
miss the party.

That sign ought to do it!

Did You Know...

Liberty is regular time off, normally weekends or holidays, not to exceed 72 hours. Sailors cannot leave the immediate area while on liberty.

Leave is earned time off. To use leave time, a sailor must put in a special request form signed off by his immediate chain of command.

Return to Colusa

April 5, 1945

Artist's Reflection:

This is a new recruit,
on liberty from boot camp.

He had his hair all cut off
and is worrying about how he looks.

He's so afraid no girls will
like him without hair
that he doesn't even
see them looking!

Did You Know...

In the 1940's, men were usually clean shaven with various styles of long hair on top, distinguished by the amount of wave and height. Many men took great pride in styling their hair.

One of the first orders of business for a new recruit was to receive a close haircut. For some, that was a blow to their self image. It took a while to see themselves as attractive in short hair.

What To Say?

October 10, 1945

Artist's Reflection:

Let's face it.

We had been at sea for months.
We were horny.

The girls looked good.

Really good!

Did You Know...

Beauty and the Beast is a fairy tale first written by French novelist Gabrielle-Suzanne Barbot de Villeneuve in 1695 and first published in 1740.

Beauty and the Beast

Undated

Artist's Reflection:

We sailors were called wolves,
but sometimes we weren't the ones
escalating romance.

This guy's a little intimidated.

Intimidated in a good way,
but nonetheless
Intimidated.

She Wolves

Undated . Guest Artists

Artist's Reflection

We spent a lot of time dreaming of women.

Guest Artist . Vixen?

*With my apologies, I don't know the name of this guest artist. I included the work in appreciation for the encouragement and camaraderie we shared. If you recognize the work, please let us know. We will credit the artist in future editions.

September 4, 1945

Artist's Reflection:

I don't think this idea
was originally mine.

As I recall, I saw something like this
involving civilians.

It was so clever I had to use the idea.

No explanation needed!

What Do You Drink?

July 10, 1945

Artist's Reflection:

Our escapades made great tales
and won the hearts of many a maiden.

War Stories are Seductive

Undated . Guest Artist

FUBAR Fun (copied for readability; not edited):

A sailor offers this version of a wartime marriage ceremony:

Chaplain: "Wilt thou, John, have this woman as they wedded wife, to live together in so far as the Bureau of Naval Personnel will allow? Wilt thou love her, comfort, honor and keep her, take her to the movies and come home promptly on all 48's?"

Man: "I will."

Chaplain: "Wilt thou, Mary, take this sailor as thy wedded husband bearing in mind liberty hours, ship schedules, restrictions, watches, sudden orders, uncertain mail conditions and various other problems of Navy life? Wilt thou obey him, love, honor and wait for him, and learn to wash, fold and press his uniforms?"

Girl: "I will."

Man: "I, John, take thee Mary as my wedded wife from 0700 to 0730, as far as permitted by my commanding officer, liberty hours subject to change without notice, for better or worse, for earlier or late, and I promise to write at least once a week."

Girl: "I, Mary, take thee John as my wedded husband, subject to the orders of the officer of the deck, changing residence whenever the ship moves, to have and to hold as long as the allotment comes through regularly, and thereunto I give thee my troth."

Chaplain: "Then let no man put usunder those whom God and the Bureau of Naval Personnel have wrought together. By virtue of the authority of Navy Regulations of the Bureau of Personnel Manual and the latest of bulletins from the Bureau of Personnel concerning matrimony, you are now man and wife, by direction of the Commanding Officer."

Guest Artist . Daydreams

*With my apologies, I don't know the name of this guest artist. I included the work in appreciation for the encouragement and camaraderie we shared. If you recognize the work, please let us know. We will credit the artist in future editions.

April 2, 1945

Artist's Reflection:

I don't know if a woman can replace a man,
but I'm quite sure
a man can't replace a woman!

Did You Know?

Over 16.5 million men and women served in the military during World War II. Of those 291,557 died in battle, 113,842 died from other causes, and 670,846 were wounded.

Approximately 400,000 women served in World War II. With the creation of the Women's Army Corps, or WAC, in 1943, women could now attain military rank and serve overseas.

Replace a Man?

Undated

Artist's Reflection

It was always bittersweet
to leave San Francisco
to go back to the South Pacific.

But we had to go.
We needed another paycheck.

Did You Know...

During World War II, the San Francisco Port of Embarkation functioned as the nerve center of a vast network of shipping facilities. During the 45 months of war, 1,647,174 passengers and 23,589,472 measured tons of cargo moved under the San Francisco Port of Embarkation into the Pacific.

Farewell San Francisco

10 Cartoons Related to The Reason We're Here

The Great War As Seen From The Navy:

We knew we were fighting a war, but we didn't dwell on it. Being in the Navy, our greatest obstacles were storms and the occasional threat of an approaching submarine. These caused concern, but to us it was more exciting than frightening. We played an important role in the war but not on the front lines.

Although we didn't fight first-hand, we saw the war's devastation when we picked up wounded from the islands. We saw enough in the wounded to know the war needed to come to an end and we could help that happen.

The Code Talkers:

We had a great gift that saved thousands of lives and shortened the war against Japan: The Code Talkers!

*The Navajo language was not written so it had to be learned in first person. They started with the Navajo language and used a number of tools to complicate it. They encrypted it and changed more than 500 words for everyday military items. They changed the code often. Navajo is a tonal language and uses many tones that aren't distinguishable in Japanese. Their code was so complex that Japan was unable to crack it. They took Navajo Sergeant Joe Kieyoomia as a POW and tortured him endeavoring to break the code. Both he and the code survived.

*Primary Source and worth reading on your own:
https://www.quora.com/Why-was-the-Navajo-code-so-hard-to-break

U.S. Marine Corps

Source: https://fronterasdesk.org/content/1005301/navajo-code-talkers-miracle-ended-world-war-ii

"I consider the Navajo Code Talkers code to be one of the great intellectual achievements of the 20th Century: the only unbroken military code of WWII!"

Author and Reporter Malcolm J. Brenner

Did You Know:

Fleming Begaye Sr., a Navajo code talker who helped the Allies gain victory in the Pacific Theater in World War II, died on May 10, 2019 at the age of 97. He was one of the last remaining members of an elite group of Navajo people who used their language to help transmit top-secret military information during the war.

The name code talkers is strongly associated with bilingual Navajo speakers specially recruited during World War II by the US Marine Corps to serve in their standard communications units of the Pacific theater. Code talking, however, was pioneered by the Cherokee and Choctaw peoples during World War I.

Did You Know...

Food, clothing, shoes, coffee, gasoline, tires, and fuel oil were rationed to the folks back home during the war. Many slogans accompanied the practice:

"Do with less so they'll have enough,"
"Be patriotic, sign your country's pledge to save the food."

Although the black market was alive and well providing these items at a higher price, most American people approved and participated in rationing. They realized their husbands, sons, and fathers were making a greater sacrifice.

**The Cover of
A Rations Book**

Rationing

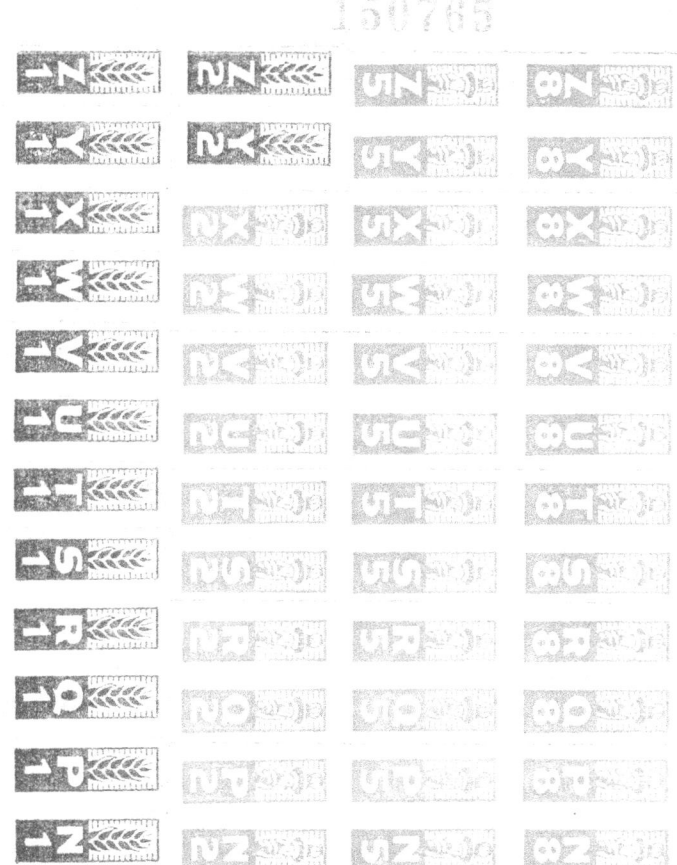

A Page of Unused Ration Stamps

September 7, 1945

Artist's Reflection:

In the heat of war,
you never know who you can trust.

They're learning Japanese.

One guy's got the book and the other is speaking it.

This guy walking by hears it and thinks,

Yikes! You guys are spies!

Did You Know...

Tokyo Rose was a name given by Allied troops in the South Pacific during World War II to all female English-speaking radio broadcasters of Japanese propaganda. The programs were broadcast in the South Pacific and North America to demoralize Allied forces abroad and their families at home by emphasizing troops' wartime difficulties and military losses.

Spies?

July 2, 1945

Artist's Reflection:

We were all aware that we were fighting a war,
but sometimes the news that we were nearing the battle
was frightening.

He's thinking of how many battle stars and ribbons he will earn.

That doesn't help his jittery nerves.

The W-W-W...War Zone

February 19, 1945

Artist's Reflection:

Guys did a lot of
gambling on board, especially
before they landed
for an invasion and
maybe get killed.

Money didn't mean a whole lot
because they might not
be alive to spend it.

Did You Know...

Ten days after the Pearl Harbor attack, Chester Nimitz was selected by President Roosevelt to be Commander and Chief of the Pacific Fleet and was promoted to Admiral. Nimitz landed at Pearl Harbor on Christmas Eve 1941. There was such a spirit of despair, dejection, and defeat you would have thought the Japanese had won the war. He immediately began building resources, morale, and a battle plan for the Pacific action.

Nimitz signed as representative for the United States when Japan formally surrendered aboard the USS Missouri on September 2, 1945.

Shooting Craps

Undated

Artist's Reflection

The water around the small islands sometimes was especially rough.

Landing troops there became a challenge.

A Little Rough

September 5, 1945

Artist's Reflection:

He's in the jungle
fighting the war,

He's trying to be really quiet.

The innocent but noisy parrot
rats him out.

He wants food.

For the Birds

Guest Artist . Undated

FUBAR Satire: Propaganda (copied for readability; not edited):

Here are quotations from radio Tokyo broadcasts for the past several years for the week beginning March 18:

March 18, 1942: "Practically entire naval strength of Allied powers has been sent to bottom by Japanese Navy. Under the circumstances, outcome of present war is crystal clear."
March 18, 1943: "Japanese Navy will control all Pacific and Indian oceans as undisputed masters."

March 19, 1942: "Americans love to take things easy and live liesurly *[sic]* lives. They have good weapons but they have no stamina and thus they flee before being able to use these weapons.
March 19, 1943: "Should United States South Pacific fleet lose vital sea battle once again in future *[sic]*, Panama Canal, Washington, Oregon, California and Australia would fall into the position of victims of Japanese attack."

March 20, 1943: "It is suicidal for antiaxis nations to retake islands now under control of Japanese forces. Antiaxis offensive against Japan is very difficult and well nigh impossible."
March 20, 1944: "Where are big bombers? Where are much publicized American Super Bombers? American boasts are being made for the sake of propaganda. There is no man in world who believes Americans are able train pilots needed fly those planes. They cannot attack Japan proper long as they do not have at their disposal bases on China coast." *[sic]*

Guest Artist . Propaganda

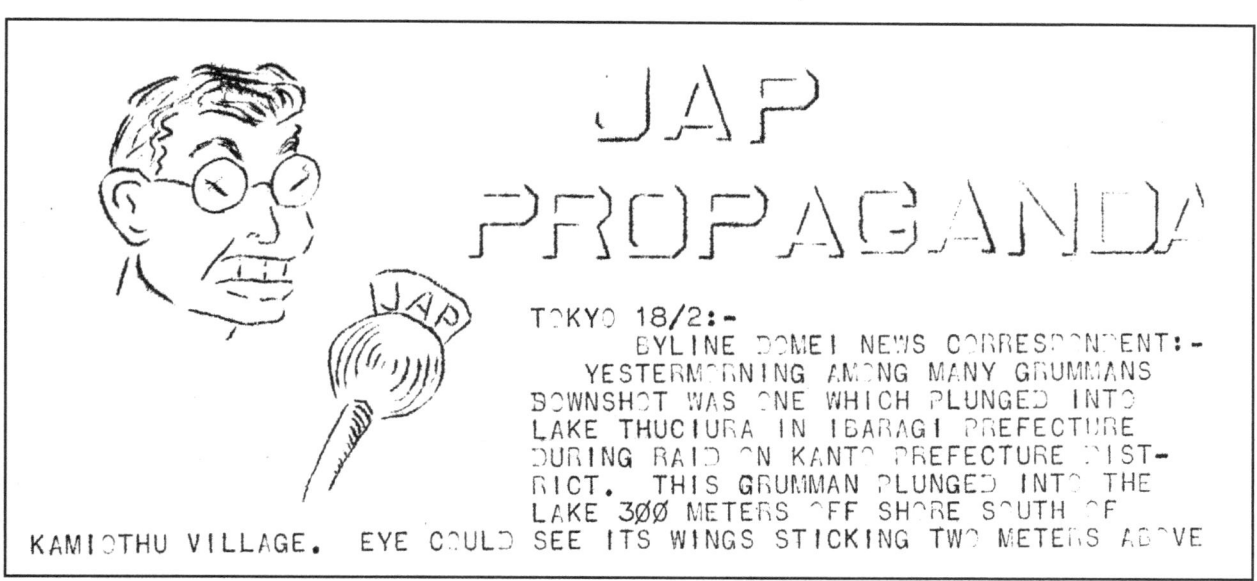

Readable Translation (not edited):

Tokyo 18/2:-
Byline dome 1 news correspondent:-
Yestermorning *[sic]* among many grummans downshot was one which plunged into Lake Thuciura in Ibaragi Prefecture during raid on Kanto Prefecture District. This grumman plunged into the lake 300 meters off shore south of Kamiothu *[sic]* Village. Eye could see its wings sticking two meters above the rippling water.

*With my apologies, I don't know the name of this guest artist. I included the work in appreciation for the encouragement and camaraderie we shared. If you recognize the work, please let us know. We will credit the artist in future editions.

August 8, 1945

Artist's Reflection:

After we dropped the bomb
I did this cartoon.
I like these guys.
I showed them with Buckeye Teeth
so you knew they were Japanese.

It wasn't intended as an insult.
It was stereotypical to distinguish their army from ours...
and to criticize them.

After all, at the time,
they were our enemies

Did You Know...

On August 6, 1945, the U.S. Army Air Forces detonated a uranium gun-type fission bomb nicknamed "Little Boy" over the Japanese city of Hiroshima.

Tokyo News

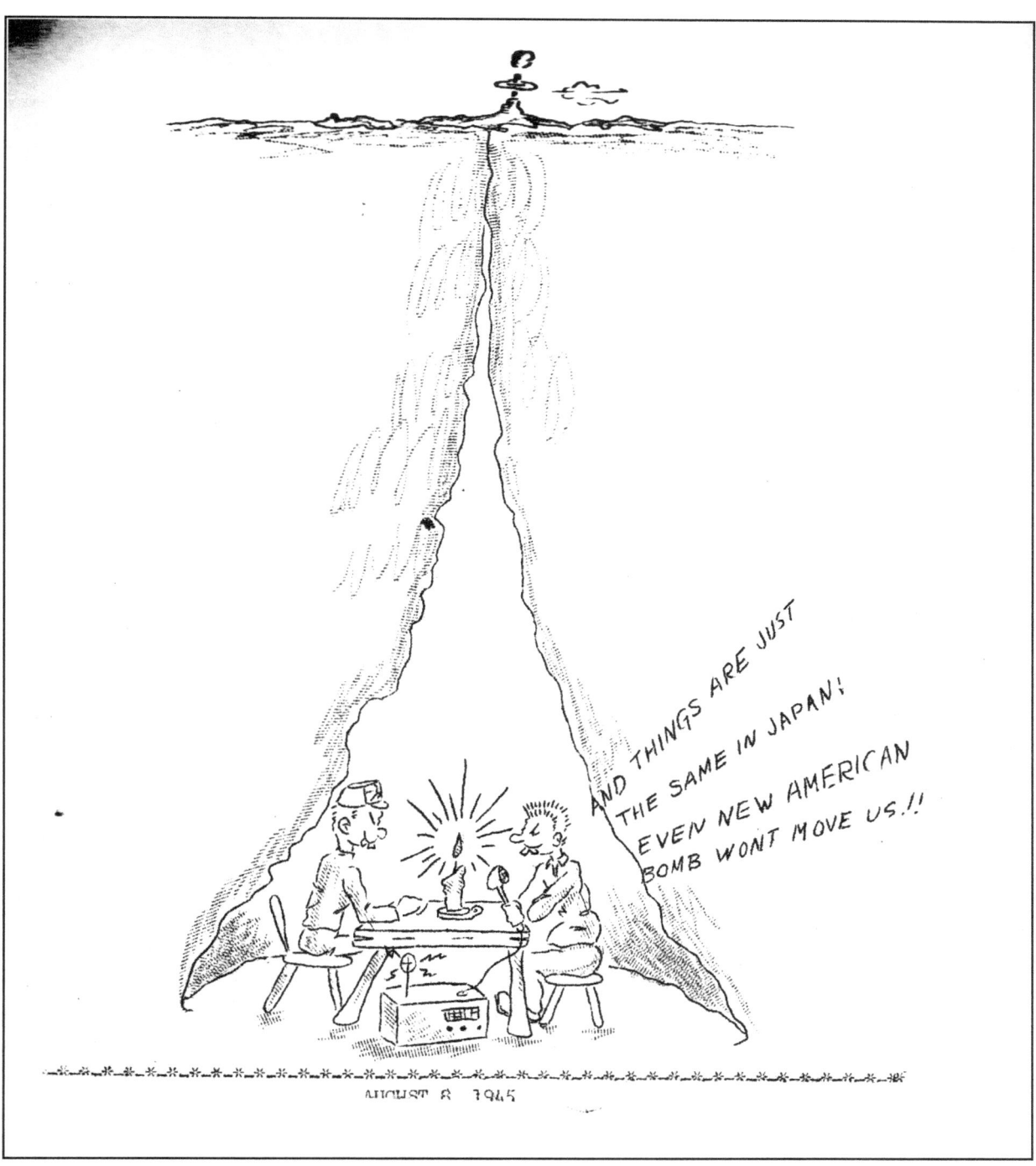

Undated

Artist's Reflection

As they listened to news

of their sinking ships,

the Japanese decided

destroying a radio

would better

boost their morale.

Did You Know...

On August 6, 1945, during World War II (1939-45), an American B-29 bomber dropped the world's first deployed atomic bomb over the Japanese city of Hiroshima. The explosion wiped out 90 percent of the city and immediately killed 80,000 people; tens of thousands more would later die of radiation exposure.

Three days later, a second B-29 dropped another A-bomb on Nagasaki, killing an estimated 40,000 people.

Japan's Emperor Hirohito announced his country's unconditional surrender in a radio address on August 15, citing the devastating power of "a new and most cruel bomb."

Japanese Radio

Undated

Artist's Reflection

Bragging rites

extended to the Japanese.

Admitting defeat was not in their nature.

Did You Know...

The surrender of Imperial Japan was announced by Hirohito on August 15 and formally signed on September 2, 1945, bringing the hostilities of World War II to a close.

Fujiyama Stands

October 16, 1945

Artist's Reflection:

The War Was Over!

Our minds had turned to

Girls,

Fun, and

Booze.

San Francisco had it all!

FUBAR Fun:

```
                    OCTOBER 16, 1945
-*-*-*-*-*-*-*-*-*-*-*-*-*-*-*-*-*-*-*-*-*-*-*-*-*-*-*-*-*-*-*-

                       --FLASH--

  WORD HAS JUST BEEN RECEIVED THAT THE COLUSA IS RETURNING TO THE
 TES. ALL YOUNG GIRLS ARE WARNED TO KEEP OFF THE STREETS AFTER DAR
  LIQUOR SHORTAGE IS EXPECTED IN THE BAY AREA----
```

Going Ashore

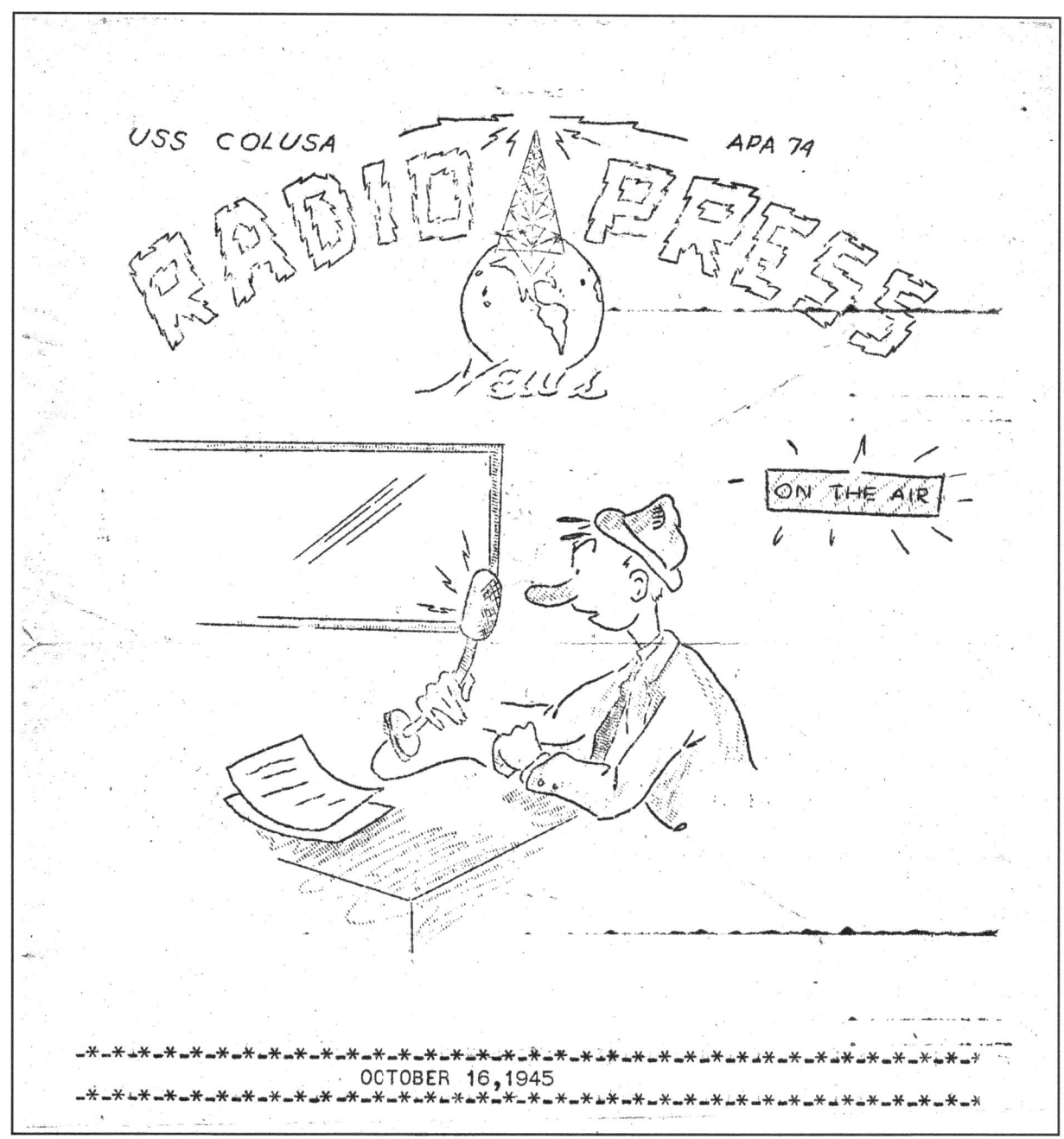

Official Telegram: The War Is Over!

```
NOS-SP—2-8-45—EM                U. S. NAVAL
                          COMMUNICATION SERVICE
                          U. S. S. COLUSA (APA-74)
```

Heading: **PRIORITY**   **ALNAV-194**   **PLAIN LANGUAGE**

ALL HANDS OF THE UNITED STATES NAVY MARINE CORPS AND COAST GUARD MAY TAKE SATISFACTION IN THE CONCLUSION OF THE WAR AGAINST JAPAN AND PRIDE IN THE PART PLAYED BY THEM IN ACCOMPLISHING THAT RESULT X PARA X THE DEMOBILIZATION OF THE ARMED FORCES OF THE UNITED STATES AND THE RETURN TO CONDITIONS OF PEACE WILL CREATE PROBLEMS TAXING PATIENCE AND CONTROL ALMOST AS GREAT AS THE TENSION OF WAR X I ASK THAT THE DISCIPLINE WHICH HAS SERVED SO WELL TO BRING THIS DEMOCRACY THROUGH HOURS OF GREAT CRISIS BE MAINTAINED TO THE END THAT NOTHING SHALL MAR THE RECORD OF ACCOMPLISHMENT AND GLORY THAT NOW BELONGS TO THE NAVY MARINE CORPS AND COAST GUARD X JAMES FORRESTAL

Date: AUGUST 14 '45 TOR 2350 Opr. WILCOX Sys. FDO: Freq. or NPM

From: SECNAV   ACTION TO: ALNAV   INFORMATION TO:

Did You Know...

The formal surrender ceremony took place aboard the Missouri in Tokyo Bay on September 2, 1945. President Truman declared V-J Day: Victory over Japan. September 2, 1945.

V-J Day Celebrations

PEARL HARBOR GLOWS IN VICTORY—This is the scene of Pearl Harbor—taken from Fleet Admiral C. W. Nimitz' rear headquarters—a few minutes after the radio report the night of 13 August that the Japanese Government had accepted the Allies' surrender terms. To the left is the Navy Yard and to the right is shown Ford Island. The pyrotechnics are from Very pistols fired from ships, and red tracer bullets. The entire harbor was a mass of color,—red, green and white—and it resembled a gigantic lighter Christmas tree. The scores of huge search-lights in the area criss-crossed the sky during the spontaneous celebration which lasted a half hour. (Official U. S. Navy Photo, Pacific.)

Occupation of Japan.

We won the war. Now it was time to take over our territory. After Japan's surrender, I was fortunate to be in the first convoy in the Occupation of Japan. We put a big task force together for the occupation. Our ship, part of the convoy, carried 900 troops to Japan, landing on Sasebo, one of the Southern Islands. It was a big convoy, and I was the Radio Operator in a boat beside the landing craft, to keep contact with our ship (just a few Navy men accompanied the Marines for the occupation). Just like you see in the movies, the front dropped down and the troops went crashing out, except the war was over then so we didn't go out shooting and fighting; we went to take over Japan.

I was in a little boat communicating with the ship while the Marines directed traffic toward the shore. Up in the hills the Japanese people were standing, watching this big convoy come in to invade their country. They hadn't lost a war in 2000 years, and here they were being occupied by the United States. They didn't know what would happen to them, but they were lined up waiting for us. My sense was that underneath an exterior that tried to seem confident, they were afraid.

Japanese watching as we docked on Sasebo to occupy their country. Photo by M. A. Lockett, August 28, 1945

Since I was in a little boat communicating between the ship and the troops, I was free to photograph our landing. What I would give if cameras then had been as good as they are now! You can see in this old photograph groups of Japanese just watching us as we landed and came ashore.

We docked. Our landing crafts were coming in. There was one Japanese kid about my age standing 40 to 50 feet away from me. He had his Japanese hat on with a star in front. It was tipped forward. I thought he was a cocky-looking guy. We were both looking at each other, and I thought, "You and I could have been good friends in different times."

World War II Key Dates:

September 1, 1939 World War II begins.
December 7, 1941 Pearl Harbor bombed.
December 8, 1941 US enters WW II.
June 6, 1944 D-Day: The Normandy invasion.
December 16, 1944 Battle of the Bulge.
April 30, 1945 Hitler commits suicide.
May 7, 1945 Germany surrenders to the allies.
August 6, 1945 Hiroshima Bombed.
August 9, 1945 Nagasaki bombed.
August 14, 1945 Japanese accept unconditional surrender.
August 28, 1945 Occupation of Japan begins
September 2, 1945 Japan formally surrenders, ending WW II.
September 3, 1945 President Truman declares VJ Day.

Note: D-Day is used routinely as military lingo for the day an operation or event will take place. For many it is also synonymous with June 6, 1944, the day the Allied powers crossed the English Channel and landed on the beaches of Normandy, France, beginning the liberation of Western Europe from Nazi control during World War II.

VJ Day: Victory over Japan.

20 Cartoons About Adjusting to Life Stateside

Homeward Bound.

We continued our duty of taking troops to and from the islands. Then we dropped the Atom Bomb, and the war was over.

After the war ended, we had a great duty! It was called "Homeward Bound." We would pick up troops and bring them back home to be discharged. Wherever we went to pick up returning servicemen, we had one day of liberty before we brought them home. I especially enjoyed getting to see Brisbane Australia on one of our trips. I bought my daughter Janene a little stuffed kangaroo with a baby in her pouch.

Me and my buddies enjoying Brisbane Australia
M. A. Lockett, 1945

Life After the Navy.

My first-born daughter Janene was born on June 11, 1945. I was many miles from home fighting the war. Mail was only received when we docked at a port (typically Manila, San Francisco, and Pearl Harbor) so she was a few days old before I knew she had been born. I carried her photo and a lock of her hair in my little photo book. It was a joy to meet her in person.

My Photo Book, Still a Treasure

After 2 1/2 years in the Navy, I was discharged on Terminal Island on February 25, 1946. Once I was discharged, I went to Disney with my drawings and they told me to go to art school. I never made it to art school. I had a wife and daughter to support. My daughter was 8 1/2 months old, and it was a privilege to finally get acquainted with her.

I lived in Lomita, worked the night shift at the Southern Counties Gas Company in San Pedro, and went to Compton College on the GI Bill. I remember working all night and going straight to school without a break. I had trouble staying awake for the lectures and exams.

While attending college, my love of drawing landed me a job as a draftsman. I earned my degree in mechanical engineering. I became a building designer and later a licensed architect. Originally all my drawings were done by hand. As technology evolved, I learned CAD (computer aided drafting). I retired at age 91 after 60 years of designing homes and businesses.

After my discharge, I never formally drew cartoons again but always "doodled" on greeting cards and scraps of paper.

March 10, 1945

Artist's Reflection:

That front ship is called the "flag,"

the boss.

He's smiling.

The other two ships are jealous

The boss…that was us.

We are the leader of the convoy.

Today we have the greatest mission!

We are bringing POWs home.

FUBAR Headlines:

```
-*-*-*-*-*-*-*-*-*-*-*-*-*-*-*-*-*-*-*-*-*-*-*-*-*-*-*-*-*-*-*-*-
                     MARCH 10, 1945
-*-*-*-*-*-*-*-*-*-*-*-*-*-*-*-*-*-*-*-*-*-*-*-*-*-*-*-*-*-*-*-*-


SAN FRANCISCO:-
                 FOR AN HOUR OR MORE TODAY THE EYES OF 272
AMERICAN ENLISTED MEN AND OFFICERS RELEASED AFTER NEARLY THREE
YEARS AS JAPANESE PRISONERS OF WAR WERE ALIGHT WITH EXCITEMENT
AT THE WELCOME GIVEN THEM BY THE PEOPLE OF SAN FRANCISCO IN BE-
HALF OF THEIR FOLKS AND THEIR COUNTRY.  THEN THEY WERE TAKEN TO
LETTERMAN HOSPITAL FOR MEDICAL CHECKUP.  THEY WILL BE OUTFITTED
THERE AND IN A FEW DAYS WILL BE ENROUTE TO THEIR HOMES ON EXTEND-
ED LEAVES AND FURLOUGHS.  OFFICIAL WELCOME TO THE RETURNING HEROES
```

Boss Ship

August 9, 1945

Artist's Reflection:

Notice the date: August 9, 1945.
Three days after we dropped the first bomb.
and the date of the second bombing.

Notice the newspaper on the floor:
Headlines show we have a new bomb.

He's looking in the catalog
planning his wardrobe
because he expects to be home soon!

FUBAR Headlines:

10 August, 1945

```
            LATEST DEVELOPMENTS
        AS OF MORNING OF 10 AUGUST

    THE NEWS OF THE JAPANESE SURRENDER OFFER WAS RECEIVED IN THE
UNITED STATES WITH WILD CHEERS.  THE NEWS ROCKED THE CAPITAL. ON
GUAM THE LONG AWAITED CELEBRATION WAS TOUCHED OFF, AND ON OKINAW
AMERICAN SOLDIERS WHO ONLY TWO MONTHS AGO CAPTURED THAT ISLAND
WENT WILD.  THEY FIRED OFF GUNS, ROCKETS, FLARES; AND TRACERS
CRISS-CROSSED IN THE SKY.  THE SOLDIERS POUNDED EACH OTHER ON TH
BACK, SHOUTING, "THE WAR IS OVER!"
```

A New Catalog

Undated

Artist's Reflection

It was time for new do's.

We had a whole new world of fashion to explore.

Looking Good

September 26, 1945

Artist's Reflection:

With the end of the war
And our days of service almost over,
Everything was changing.

Prints Are In

September 27, 1945

Artist's Reflection:

War stories take on a life of their own.

Did You Know...

*World War II veterans tend to enjoy bragging about the fact they spent time in "The Great War" and telling their stories…their happy or adventurous stories, that is. But the real horror of battle wasn't often discussed. Many families will never know what their loved ones experienced; some World War II vets, these many years later, are just beginning to talk.

Soldiers returning from Vietnam were diagnosed with PTSD (Post Traumatic Stress Disorder) causing night terrors, heavy drinking, survivor's guilt, depression, exaggerated startle responses, profound and lingering sadness. The diagnosis that became widely known was assumed to be unique to veterans of Vietnam. "Bad war, bad outcome, bad aftereffects," is the way historian Thomas Childers put it.

World War II veterans know better. It was referred to by other names: shell shock, combat fatigue, neuropsychiatric disorders. In the immediate postwar years, the press was full of woeful tales. But with the passage of time and the prevailing male ethos — the strong, silent type — World War II was soon overshadowed by the Cold War and eventually Vietnam.

*Source: Tim Madigan, The Washington Post, September 11, 2015: https://www.washingtonpost.com/opinions/the-greatest-generations-forgotten-trauma/2015/09/11/8978d3b0-46b0-11e5-8ab4-c73967a143d3_story.html?noredirect=on&utm_term=.c36b15464fbb

Bragging Rites

Undated

Artist's Reflection

I got in trouble with my
commanding officer for this one.

On leave in San Francisco,
we enjoyed visiting Finocchio's*
and watching guys impersonating girls.
That inspired this cartoon.

When the paper came out, the captain came
running into the Radio Room.
He was not happy!

*Finocchio's was a popular tourist attraction, a bar featuring men performers dressed as women, active in San Francisco between 1929 and 1999.

Did You Know?

- During World War II, gays were not allowed in the military.
- A complete ban of gays was put into writing in 1982.
- It was replaced by "don't ask; don't tell" in 1993.
- In 2010, gays were openly welcomed to join the military.

What's Next?

[sic]

September 21, 1945

Artist's Reflection:

The war is over.
He's enjoying some R and R.

On the floor is the bucket of wine.
His drink's on the table and
he's kind of blurry.

No thoughts of the war.

His imagination is running wild...
The Colusa as a "Luxury Cruise Ship."

Did You Know...

R and R is military slang for Rest & Relaxation time. A soldier on active duty must be approved by the commanding officer to take a leave.

Island Leisure

FUBAR Dreams:

```
*-*-*-*-*-*-*-*-*-*-*-*-*-*-*-*-*-*-*-*-*-*-*-*-*-*-*-*-*-*-*-*-*-*-*-*-*-
SS COLUSA              SEPTEMBER 21, 1945                        APA 74
*-*-*-*-*-*-*-*-*-*-*-*-*-*-*-*-*-*-*-*-*-*-*-*-*-*-*-*-*-*-*-*-*-*-*-*-*-

     THE COLUSA, THE SHIP THAT SERVED SO WELL DURING THE WAR, OFFERS
 OU HER SERVICES NOW IN TIME OF PEACE.  CRUISE THE BEAUTIFUL BLUE
 ACIFIC, ENJOYING LIFE TO THE FULL IN HER LUXURIOUSLY FURNISHED QUAR-
 E S.
     WE OFFER YOU PEACE, REST, PLEASURE AND A FULL DAY WITH PLEASANT
 OMPANIONS.
     FRESH HOT AND COLD RUNNING WATER ARE CONTINUOUSLY AT YOUR DIS-
 OSAL.  THE FOOD IS OF UNEXCELLED QUALITY PREPARED BY THE FINEST COOKS
 ND BAKERS IN THE PACIFIC.
```

Undated, Guest Artist*

Artist's Reflection

Since we were a transport ship,
we spent time with
the other branches of service.

Although there was friendly competition,
we were comrades in arms
and appreciated one another.

The fellow who drew this was a passenger
on our transport.
He had previously worked for Disney
and encouraged me to apply there
after my discharge.

I did, and they told me to go
to art school.

*With my apologies, I don't know the name of this guest artist. I included the work in appreciation for the encouragement and camaraderie we shared. If you recognize the work, please let us know. We will credit the artist in future editions.

Guest Artist . Thanks from the Marines

July 8, 1945

Artist's Reflection:

This is me.

When I went overseas,
my wife was pregnant.

When I came back home
she had a flat belly
and we had a baby on the floor,
Janene, my first-born.
She was 8 1/2 months old when I met her.
It was love at first sight.

I'm ready to make another baby.

The Homecoming

September 18, 1945

Artist's Reflection:

On the ship,
all of our belongings fit in one
canvas bag...
clothes and everything else.

This guy's been discharged and is
getting his delivery...

double boxes, aircraft gear, radios...
all kinds of stuff.
They're unloading the truck.

What's left on the ship?

Special Delivery

Undated

Artist's Reflection:

The old slogan
"Absence makes the heart grow fonder"
is often a myth.

Too many servicemen returned home
to find they had been replaced;
too many wives had to face
the reality and aftermath of
their servicemen's infidelity.

Did You Know?

Marriage rates increased 250% after the Selective Service Act was passed. After the draft, marriage rates increased another 25%
After Pearl Harbor, rates rose 60% higher than the same month the previous year.

With quick marriages came rising divorce rates as well. Between 1940 and 1944, divorce rates rose from 16 per 100 marriages to 27 per 100 marriages.

One in six marriages ended in divorce in 1940; one in four marriages ended in divorce in 1946. Because men were marrying women they hardly knew before leaving for war, there was little time to build a relationship. Infidelity, prostitution and women abandoning their husbands for lovers was at an all-time high.

Source: https://familiesatwar2014.wordpress.com/2014/03/23/world-war-ii-marriage-and-divorce/

Surprise!

September 20, 1945

Artist's Reflection:

In the Navy, clothes were hung with little string ties.
There were no clothes pins.

Back home, he is helping with the laundry.

She doesn't know why he didn't
use the clothes pins.

What Are These?

Undated

Artist's Reflection:

When we returned home after the war,
we took much of our training
and lingo with us.

Our children didn't always know...
or obey...
our commands.

They quickly learned, however, that "chow"
meant they got to eat!

Taking Control

Undated

Artist's Reflection

A yeoman was a secretary on the ship.
Everything was submitted in 7 copies.

This guy carries it a little too far...
He's in the process of making
seven copies of kids!

I like this guy!

Did You Know...

A yeoman was a service member within the US Navy that performed administrative work as his primary assignment.

Seven Copies, Please

Undated

Artist's Reflection

He thought home would be leisure,
like a full-time leave.

On the ship he had four hours on
and four hours off.

Now he's home walking the baby
and she's sleeping.

Four hour watch, just like on the ship.

No leisure for me.

Did You Know?

Children were often forgotten victims of war...
- children who became war orphans;
- children born while their father was away;
- children, the product of soldiers' relationships with local women, outcast by their society;
- children abandoned by their father when he returned home from war.

It Ain't Over

September 28, 1945

Artist's Reflection:

I made up the poem:

On the upper left you've got a
couple sitting on a park bench.

Then they got married; see the wedding cake.

Then they have a little kid.
He's having to walk the floor
in the middle of the night.

At 3 o'clock in the morning
he's getting ready to re-enlist in the Navy
so he doesn't have to walk the baby
while his wife sleeps.

Enlist Today

Undated

Artist's Reflection

He's back home and
wanting to forget the war.

Even back home,
even though it was morale building,
you couldn't get away from
the sound of G. I. Jill!

Did You Know...

G. I. Jill was Martha Wilkerson, the disc jockey host of G. I. Jive, a musical radio program on the Armed Forces Radio Service. She is credited with bringing positive morale and was the number one overseas attraction during World War II. By the end of January, 1945, she had made 870 broadcasts.

No Rest

Undated

Artist's Reflection

It is good to be home!

It was a great experience.

75 Years Later
I continue to reap benefits
through the Veterans Administration.

It was an awesome experience.
I would do it again.

No Thanks!

Undated

Artist's Reflection

It's a good time
to dream
new dreams!

But beware!
Birds are flying overhead
and taxes are on the rise!

From The President

Undated

Artist's Reflection

We are closed.

This guy is leaving the John.

He wiped and tossed the paper.

End of Press!
End of War!

Time to begin a new life.

Did You Know...

The USS Colusa was commissioned on December 20, 1944. She was decommissioned May 16, 1946. She was scrapped March 2, 1966.

She was my home for 2 1/2 years. She holds a lifetime of memories.

End of Press

About the Cartoonist

Milton Ambrose Lockett was born in St. Louis, Missouri on November 11, 1926. He graduated from Narbonne High School in Lomita, California and attended nearby Compton College.

Milt is proud to be a World War II Navy veteran. His ship, the USS Colusa, was a troop transport ship. They delivered new troops to the battlefield and picked up wounded to return home or to hospitals. Although he wasn't involved directly in combat, he saw its first-hand devastation in the lives of the wounded. He also saw first-hand the rewards of his service as part of the first troops to occupy Japan.

Milt came from a patriotic family. His parents signed for him to enlist in the Navy at age 17; his older brother, Ray, was also in the Navy. Throughout their lives, they shared pride and memories of their times in service to America.

Ray Lockett
US Navy, 1943

Milton Lockett
US Navy, 1945

Brothers, Proud Veterans
Ray and Milt, 2010

Milt came home from the war to support his growing family while he attended Compton College on the G. I. Bill and worked at various jobs, usually in the design industry. Eventually he became a California Registered Building Designer and then a California Licensed Architect. He has been in the building design and architect field for over 62 years. He started out doing hand drawings and creating blueprints in his office. His children sometimes enjoyed coloring the homes he designed for his pleased clients. When computers were introduced to the industry, he was an eager learner and switched to CAD (Computer Assisted Design).

He was an active member of the American Institute of Building Design and served as president for AIBD and the Architectural Designers Association. He is a former member of the City of Garden Grove Administrative Board of Appeals. His motto is "designed as you like it." His designs range from ultra-modern to Victorian because he is talented in listening to and customizing his work to meet the owner's expectations.

Milt was a radio operator and cartoonist for the ship's newspaper. His cartoons served to boost morale during the tough times of World War II. He and his wife, Sharon Marshall Lockett, were both inducted into the Youth-on-the-Move, Inc. International Educators' Hall of Fame, in 2017. For his service, he received the Military Honors Award.

Milton Lockett
International Educators'
Hall of Fame
Military Honors
2017

Sharon Marshall Lockett
International Educators'
Hall of Fame Inductee
2017

Milt has been blessed with four children, four step-children, six grandchildren, nine great-grandchildren, and four great-great grandchildren.

**Milt with his four children
Mel, Lisa, Janene, Milt, Gary
90th Birthday Party
November 11, 2016**

Milt and his wife Sharon reside in Laguna Niguel, California. Although retired, his designs may be viewed on his web site:

        www.malockettbuildingdesign.com

His work is published by Lockett Learning Systems:

        www.lockettlearningsystems.com

www.ingramcontent.com/pod-product-compliance
Lightning Source LLC
Chambersburg PA
CBHW081744100526
44592CB00015B/2287